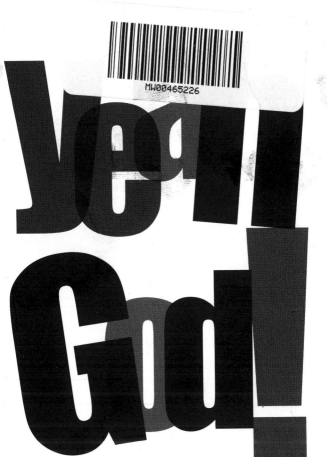

Yeah God!

George Potts Young

"With faith in it's smallest form, you still have enough power to move the earth."
-George Potts Young

This is dedicated to every person who needs restoration, revelation, or a restart while on the journey of life. I pray that something in these next few pages will encourage and inspire you to keep going. No matter how it feels, there's always one person on the journey with you... God.

Table of Contents

Table of Contents (cont'd)

PREFACE
Perfect People Shouldn't...

Perfect people shouldn't write books! I almost didn't write this, because I didn't feel qualified, which is the very thing that has stopped so many people from living in purpose. YOU ARE QUALIFIED by God to inherit all that he has for you. Your imperfections and experiences, are what prepare you; they birth godly revelation, which ultimately produces wisdom in you.

I will not lie and say that this book will take away all of your struggles. You will begin this book with some type of struggle, and you will end this book with some type of struggle. Struggle is a part of life, but you have victory over every struggle! In life, you will fight, but with God, you will win!

I want to help you restart. In order to restart, you must first renew. Renew your mind, your lifestyle, your conversations, and everything else that you regularly do. Many of us aren't where we want to be in life, because God isn't where He needs to be in our lives. We must fight to transform! There are so many things that influence us and our way of thinking, even in how we think about God. Everything we ingest from music to social media affects us. We must change our spiritual and emotional appetites, to reflect who God says we are. It's just like eating. Everything you put in your body either helps or hurts you.

God is available and accessible to anyone, anywhere, and at anytime. God has given us inspiration in the form of nature, music, animals, and humanity. There is no shortage of it. If you're looking to be inspired, you don't have to look far, just look up.

There's no better time than now to embark on a new spiritual journey. Every day you wake up, spend your first minutes with God! I pray that the next 31 days of your life are filled with prayer, faith, and expectation of what God has promised you!

Do not conform to the
pattern of this world, but
be transformed by the
renewing of your mind.
Then you will be able to test
and
approve what God's will is...
his good, pleasing and
perfect will.
Romans 12:2

be renewed & transformed.

Big God,
Big You.

Genesis 1:27 - Made in His image...

You are more like God than you think. As a child, I couldn't fathom the idea of being like God. How can little me be like big Him? Knowing that God made me, using himself as the mold, puts new meaning to "who I am." Everything that God is, we have the ability to be, but only when we make the choice to be "like Him."

If we compare ourselves to God, we will feel as small as small gets. However, when we carry God inside of us, we instantly become big. Can something big be inside of something small? John 4:4 says, "Greater is He who is in me, than he that is in the world." This means that when we have God inside of us, there is nothing more powerful than we are.

The bible says, "despise not small beginnings." Everything BIG that we see, started as a small thought, idea, or seed inside of someone, and has manifested into what we see today. God often used young or small people to do big things.

In John 6:9, a little boy's lunch fed more than 5,000 people, young(little) David killed Goliath the giant, and Gideon's small army defeated the Midianites, who outnumbered them greatly.

Here are a few things to remember for this upcoming month:

1. Don't look at what you don't have, and don't underestimate what you do have.
2. Just because it didn't work for them, doesn't mean it won't work for you. Do what God tells you to do.
3. Don't let powerful/influential people intimidate you, or make you feel ill equipped for your journey. God called you. He will only send you where he has already been and prepared for your arrival.
4. When God leads you to do something that you feel unprepared for, trust Him. He will either prepare you on the journey, or you already have everything you need.

I can only imagine how many times people felt ill equipped to fight in the bible days. However, God always seemed to use the "little" to win! There's an old saying that says, "little becomes much in the master's hands."

Moses had a rod and parted the red sea. David used one stone and defeated a giant. Paul and Silas prayed and praised, they shook the entire earth, and everyone's chains were released. You have more than you think. Everything you have, God will show you how to use, so you can get to your next season.

Prayer

Dear God,
I thank you for giving me identity. I'm made in your image,
and that means I can overcome
anything that this day brings.
Help me to see you, when I see
myself. I am fearfully and won-
derfully made, crafted with
greatness in mind. Today, I will
remember John 4:4. I know that
if you are in me, I can defeat
anything outside of me.

In Jesus' Name,
Amen.

Big Purposes, Small Packages:

You'll grow into it.

The question that has caused many tears, stressful days, and sleepless nights... "WHY AM I HERE?" We all have questioned our purpose and wondered when we would actually find it. The problem isn't finding purpose, the problem is believing in purpose; believing that where you are at this very moment, is a part of your purpose.

What is purpose? Purpose is God's intended outcome for your life and existence. It all begins with God. The only way to know the purpose of a thing, is to know the creator of that thing.

A year ago, a friend of mine gave birth. As I sat through her baby shower, several people bought clothes that were too big for her newborn. Perplexed, I began to ask myself, "why buy something that can't be worn now?"

I asked my friend, and she responded

with such a simple answer, "the baby will grow into it." My spiritual light bulb went off and it all made sense. We are all born in to this world with a full grown purpose that doesn't fit yet, but we will grow into it.

How many times have you been intimidated by the size of your dream, idea, or vision? Don't allow the size of what God has shown you, to cause doubt in you. If your vision isn't too big for you, it's too small for God. A big vision is a sign that it's from God.

One of my favorite scriptures is Jeremiah 1:5, "before I formed you in the womb, I knew you..." It lets us know that God began working on our purposes, far before we were ever introduced to the world.

Not only did he know us, God also knew the plans for our lives. Our job is to follow the plan that we can't see. How? By faith.

Prayer

Dear God,
Thank you for crafting me with a beautiful purpose. I rebuke everything that will try to make me doubt you, or my purpose. Give me the faith I need to continue growing, and walking in my calling. I pray that I will experience joy and excitement in each stage of my purpose, and never intimidated by the size of it. I know that you will complete everything that you have started in me!

In Jesus' Name,
Amen.

For I know the plans I have for you... plans to prosper you and not to harm you, plans to give you hope and a future.
Jeremiah 29:11

Yeah God! (The Devotional)

Whatcha' Looking For?
Find Faith.

Many people say they are looking for God, but they are actually searching for faith in God. We don't have to look for God, because he's never lost. All we have to do is accept him. However, finding faith is an intentional journey, that isn't always easy.

There were three steps I took to find my faith. First, I prayed and never stopped. Matthew 7:7 says to seek and find. I talked to God like he was my friend. I told him my feelings, my fears, my confusion, and my desire to know him. The bible promises that we will find what we seek.

Secondly, I was careful of my conversations. I realized that much of what I believed, could be traced back to what I listened to the most. Romans 10:17 says, "... faith comes by hearing, and hearing by the word of God." If I listen to anything other than the word of God, I will start believing that. A ship doesn't sink because of all the water that surrounds it, it sinks because of the water that gets inside of it. Your mind is the ship. If you allow anything other than God to get inside, you are destined to start sinking.

Lastly, I learned to let go. A big part of faith is learning to relinquish your need to understand everything. You will never understand everything. Faith doesn't try to micromanage God, faith affords you peace, even when you don't understand.

Faith, just like anything else, has to become a lifestyle. It is a seed. When you water it, it will grow. Practice letting go. Practice trusting God. It is the foundation of being a Christian, and it is proof that even what you can't see, still exists.

Prayer

Dear God,
Help me to trust you and your word. I desire for my faith to grow, and for the residue of fear and doubt to dissipate. I release my illusion of control, and relinquish my ways to you, in exchange for your peace. My ultimate desire is to please you, and to live a purposeful life built on healthy faith.

In Jesus' Name,
Amen.

Now faith is the substance of things hoped for, the evidence of things not seen.
Hebrews 11:1

Yeah God! (The Devotional)

The Waiting Room

Give Me Eyes For My Journey Only

Who likes waiting? Have you ever been in a waiting room at a doctor's office, a salon, or maybe even the place that we all hate to wait, the DMV? What about waiting long, and someone who arrived after you, gets called before you? That is annoying!

The waiting room of life can be similar. You work hard, trying to do everything right, and everyone else seems to get called or "blessed" before you. Maybe you're waiting for a new car, a new house, or a new job, and you still haven't received it yet. It can be hard to find peace in this part of the process. It can also be hard to be happy for others.

My advice? First, make sure you're not waiting on God to do something that he has already given you the power to do on your own. There's nothing like waiting, and once they call your name they say, "you could've done this online." Lol. Not funny!

But seriously, how many times have we waited on God to do things, that we already had instructions on?

Secondly, don't watch the clock. Watching the clock is our way of measuring how long it's taking, but God's clock is different. It does nothing but aggravate you and distract you from experiencing peace. Clocks can only show time that has passed, it can't show seeds that were sown, nor can it show how close you are to your purpose. Clocks can be misleading.

Thirdly, don't envy someone else's position in line. You don't know what condition they have. For example, in an emergency room, the condition dictates the position. A person who came in with an extreme issue, will be seen before those with lesser problems. Envying their position, may cause you to end up with their condition.

Lastly, keep an attitude of humility and gratefulness while you wait. God still wants you to experience him in the waiting room. Frustration can prevent you from enjoying the fullness of his presence.

One of the first bible verses I learned, was Isaiah 40:31. "But they that wait upon the lord shall renew their strength..." It teaches us that waiting produces strength, the ability to fly high, and the ability to move at any pace without getting tired or being defeated.

God has a plan for you and it has an appointed time. Until then, find enjoyment... even in the process. Don't wait until your name is called to be happy! You can experience God's joy now. You won't regret the wait!

Prayer

Dear God,
I pray for everyone in the waiting room of life. I pray that they will experience peace while waiting. I will wait on you, because I know that the wait is a part of my purpose and plan. If I feel discouraged, I pray that my faith will recognize your overwhelming love for me, and remind me that you are still working. I will not let the enemy confuse me into thinking that the wait is a sign of failure. Instead, I will be grateful and anticipate the manifestation of my blessing.

In Jesus' Name,
Amen.

Fill In The Blanks
What's The Answer?

How many times have you felt like something was missing, but didn't know what that something was? When I was in school, many lessons required filling in the blanks. However, there was no way to fill in the blanks, without reading the entire sentence. The sentence gave context clues, which helped formulate the answer.

The bible is the context of God and life. Those blanks that you are looking to fill, God is the answer, and his word gives the context clues.

When I was young, I remember my momma always saying, "there's nothing new under the sun." Everything we encounter to-day, God provided answers and solutions to back then. There's nothing new or surprising to God.

What's missing is only scary when you don't know where to find the answer. In life, we'll be tested. However, life is an open book test. The bible is always available for you to find answers, and fill in your blanks. This doesn't mean it will always make sense, sometimes the blank just needs to be filled with faith.

I don't know what blank needs to be filled for you, but I know that God specializes in filling in what's missing. He's the teacher, but he's also the student inside of you, when you carry him with you.

Prayer

Dear God,
I thank you for filling in every gap in my life. When I have questions, I know that you have the answers. You said that you will perfect everything that concerns me, so I trust in your ability to provide the solution. Today, I will walk in confidence, knowing that you have already filled the blank, before I knew I needed it filled. You are the answer.

In Jesus' Name,
Amen.

Yeah God! (The Devotional)

On vs Forward
Where Are You Moving?

Moving on and moving forward sound the same, but they aren't. Moving on is inevitable. Time automatically moves us on. Moving forward is only done with peace. It requires God's strength, and our healthy response to whatever the situation is.

The good part about moving forward is that you don't have to wait on apologies from those who have hurt you, you don't need the approval of those around you, and you don't have to wait until the tears or pain stop, you can move forward immediately. We've all experienced disappointments, however, you choose what to do with your lessons and experiences. Choose to move.

The most important thing in moving forward, is moving with integrity. Don't be forced to turn around after you've already began to move forward. How you choose to move, determines where you get to move.

I resigned from a job years ago, and there were a lot of requirements and loose ends that still existed on my last day of employment. I was faced with the dilemma of still ensuring they would be tied, or letting go and not caring. I chose to let go, and not care. I was ready to move forward. However, I actually only moved on.

It took me years to turn around and handle what I should have done initially. I learned a great lesson. I owed it to myself and my purpose, to move forward with no side effects and without the possibility of being forced to turn around.

I prayed and asked God for direction, and finally I was able to turn around and tie the loose ends. Although I could've saved time and skipped some scars by handling it in the beginning, God's grace still covered me in the end.

In life, we will constantly be faced with situations that require choices. Learn to make wise decisions based off of where you want to go, not where you currently are. In order to walk into the new, you must first walk out of the old properly.

Prayer

Dear God,
Thank you for the grace to move forward from any situation that life presents to me. I know that the only way to move forward, is to include you in every step of my process. Because I know you are working behind the scenes, I will respond to my situations with your godly love. You desire for me to move in integrity. Therefore, I exchange my need for understanding and apologies, for your direction and peace. You are my restorer!

In Jesus' Name,
Amen.

Yeah God! (The Devotional)

The Other WTF:

Weapons That Form

We have all probably heard the scripture, "no weapon formed against me shall prosper…" However, when weapons form, do we realize they're weapons? Do we really believe that they won't prosper? If so, why are we so offended, embarrassed, and sometimes ashamed when we come face to face with a weapon?

2017 was a very interesting year for me. I encountered a weapon formed against me by a "friend" The weapon tried to kill my character, my reputation, and even future career opportunities. However, I decided to be fearless, unashamed, and actually encouraged by it. Encouraged by a weapon? Yes, encouraged!

A weapon only has the power we give to it. Weapons create fear, doubt, stress, and shame, but a weapon can not kill you. It can only create more weapons within you, if you allow it.

People waste time forming weapons that won't be usable. They form the weapons, but the Holy Spirit puts the safety on the weapon. God is in control. There's no reason to be fearful of someone else's power or weapon in your life. People can't do anything other than what God allows them to do.

Prayer

Dear God,
Thank you for your protection.
I realize that I will have to face
circumstances in my life, however, I don't have to fear the outcome. I have no reason to fear,
because you said in your word,
that you are always with me.
You are my strength, your are my
present help, and you will always
cause me to win!

In Jesus' Name,
Amen.

Yeah God! (The Devotional)

The Recipe for Purpose:
All Things Work Together

Everything that is created must go through a process. Don't be discouraged by your process. While your journey may require some sacrifice from you, it will never amount to the pain of the cross. Jesus paid the price a long time ago. Our payment for purpose is the process.

When I was a kid, I loved Christmas time, because I knew my mom would be making her famous butter cookies. I would stand in the kitchen while she mixed the ingredients, and I would taste them. I couldn't understand why separately the ingredients were "nasty", but mixed together and baked, they were amazing.

Individually, ingredients, events, seasons, situations, failed relationships, etc might not feel good, but once they're all added in, and you're done processing, the end product is good!

Every time there's a shift or transi-

tion, there will be a process. The purpose
of the process is to ensure that a product is
built to last and strong enough to maintain
it's quality, throughout it's lifetime.

Romans 8:28, says "...all things work
together for good to them that love God, to
them who are the called according to his
purpose." While all of your life ingredients
are being mixed, don't worry. If it's not good
yet, that means "all things" are not done
working.

Prayer

Dear God,
I know that my process is the
only way for you to prepare me
and condition me for what you
created me to do. I pray that
you will continue to give me the
strength I need, to go through the
process and to come out the best
finished product. I realize that
everything in my life is used by
you, to make me the best version
of me that I can be. The heat of
my process will not cause me to
give up. As you lead me, I will
follow you.

In Jesus' Name,
Amen.

Yeah God! (The Devotional)

No Limits...
Just Boundaries

If we're honest, we've all felt limited by God at some point. Maybe we've felt limited by God's instructions to us, maybe it was God's requirement of being patient, or maybe even God's direction to put someone else's needs first. Whatever it is, feeling limited or restrained, doesn't feel good, but what if I told you that God is incapable of limiting who He created?

God doesn't set limits, he sets boundaries. Boundaries are set to protect us while moving forward, but limits are set to prevent us from moving forward. God's goal is for us to fulfill the purpose for which we were created and formed.

A good creator has standards, expectations, and instructions for their creation to be productive and successful. There's an expected outcome for each of us, and God wants to ensure that we reach it.

The enemy sets limits. Those limits

can be through our thoughts, our speech, and our actions. He will present us bad decisions disguised as "freedom", but in reality, it's his way of keeping us bound, and away from what God wants for us. The faux freedom that the enemy presents, will leave you feeling guilty, condemned, and feeling like a failure.

In John 14:12, Jesus told us we would do "greater works" than him. That is a clear reminder, that we were designed to live our lives without limits. We were made in God's image, that includes his unlimited power. He didn't give us power to do greater, just to turn around and limit us from being greater.

Even when it feels like you're being held back, realize that God's boundaries are to protect, produce, and promote us in purpose, on purpose. We don't see, think, or know in the way that God does. Trust your creator, and trust His word. He can do exceeding abundantly above all that you could ask or think, there are no limits!

Prayer

Dear God,
Thank you for taking the limits off of my mind, my heart,
and my spirit. You've given me
the strength to not submit to the
world's way of freedom, and to
recognize what liberty is in you.
Your will for my life is that I
prosper and be of good health.
I'm thankful for the boundaries
you've set to protect me from the
adversary, to produce purpose
in me, and to promote me to my
next season.

In Jesus' Name,
Amen.

Yeah God! (The Devotional)

Throw The Whole Ruler Away

Purpose Can't Be Measured

In today's time, we are made aware of everyone, what they have, what they do, and what they think. Between social media, blogs, and television, we are constantly faced with either being enough, not enough, or too much.

Society is a big ruler by which everyone is measured. Throw it away. You can not measure your purpose using someone else's purpose or life as the ruler. We weren't created to compete, instead, the goal is to complete. Each of us have a different plan and purpose. Our journeys will differ, but they will connect and fit together like puzzle pieces.

Every day, I ask God to give me eyes for my journey only. This prayer continues to protect me from comparing my life, my path, and my purpose to others. Why would you want a person to set your standard of achievement? God's plan is for you to exceed what your mind can think, and what your eyes can see.

I learned that watching others too closely, robs you of your individuality, uniqueness, and the ability to notice the moments in your own life that deserve celebrating. Don't limit your potential by setting your standards according to others.

Pay careful attention to your own work, for then you will get the satisfaction of a job well done, and you won't need to compare yourself to anyone else.
Galatians 6:4

Prayer

Dear God,
Thank you for giving me eyes
for my journey only. I have confidence in you and your ability to manifest my purpose. So
instead of comparing my life to
those around me, I will focus on
he standard you have set for me.
While I continue on this journey,
I will celebrate purpose in other
people's lives. Thank you for re-
minding me that there is enough
purpose to go around for all of us.
I have no reason to be envious or
jealous of anyone.

In Jesus' Name,
Amen.

Yeah God! (The Devotional)

I HAD A DREAM

...but what happened to it?

One of the best gifts in the world is the ability to dream. God used dreams many times in the bible, to give information, warnings, and encouragement. Dreams not only offer insight, they can also give you prophetic glimpses of the future.

Visions and dreams are somewhat the same, the only difference is your physical state. A vision occurs with you awake, while dreams happen in your sleep. So many of us have had dreams and visions that have either scared us, or intimidated us, and because of that, our dreams and vision died.

There are three things that I call dream killers. First, there is being half-hearted. With anything, commitment is the beginning of being productive and effective. You must stay consistent in the work you do towards your dream. You must have faith in God, and do the work.

The second dream killer is indecisiveness. I will never forget having a conversation with my mentor. He called me to present me a great offer, I responded, "I will pray about it." He responded and said, "That's a cop out." Lol. It was true. I used that as a way to not make a decision immediately. Now, I'm not saying that we shouldn't pray, but how many times have you known the right thing to do, but out of fear, you needed to "pray" about it to buy more time.

Finally, don't repeat what your critics say. While critics can say helpful things, if it's not done in a constructive way, it can be destructive.

When I performed at Coachella with Beyoncé, she said something that was simple, but has stayed with me. In reference to some people saying it was going to be impossible for her to pull off a show of the magnitude, her response was that if God gave her a vision for it, she knew somehow it could be done. God will never show you something that can't be accomplished. He will bring it to pass.

Prayer

Dear God,
Thank you for the vision that you've given to me. I declare that I will be a good steward over every dream & vision you give to me. I know that if you've shown it to me, you have the ability to bring it to pass. Help me to not be intimidated by the size of my dream, by re-minding me of how big you are. I pray that my vision and work will inspire others to dream big, and trust big!

In Jesus' Name,
Amen.

Yeah God! (The Devotional)

Much Is Required

...even by your enemies

We don't wrestle against flesh and blood, so why do we waste so much energy and time fighting people? God wants to bless you. What if I told you that God wants you to be a blessing to your enemies, too? I remember the first time God instructed me to bless my enemy, I was like, "Nah God, I'm good!" Lol. What's the benefit? Blessings.

To whom much is given, much is required. God doesn't bless us to make others feel bad or small. Yes, even with those that we may have an issue with, God is always calling us to treat them with the same love, grace, and mercy that he has freely given us.

It's up to you to break any cycles of hatred and anger that surrounds you. The only way to overcome evil, is with good. 1 Peter 3:9 promises us that we will inherit a blessing, when we repay evil with blessings, and not insult. How we respond also reveals the condition of our hearts.

Pride makes you pay them back, but

but purpose makes you pray them back to God, to healing, and to restoration. Proverbs 16:7 says, "When a man's ways please the LORD, he maketh even his enemies to be at peace with him." That's God's plan... us at peace with those we encounter.

Prayer

Dear God,
I know that my fight with people, is a spiritual fight, and requires spiritual responses. When I seemingly forget your grace towards me, remind me, so that I may show others that same grace. You have directed me to love and pray for my enemies, so I will follow your lead in how to love and overcome evil. Thank you for blessing me in spite of what I've done, I will continue to be a blessing to others, in spite of what they've done towards me. I want to be the best representative of your love that I can be.

In Jesus' Name,
Amen.

Yeah God! (The Devotional)

The Personal Trainer
Getting Your Spirit In Shape

Last year, I started working out, and initially, I hated it! It was so intimidating. The people, the weights, the monthly fee... intimidating. Lol! After a week or two, I started finding joy in the process, because I saw minor results. There was one workout I hated though, DIPS! I couldn't do them. I wasn't strong enough to do them. I tried, and tried, but never could do more than one. After that, I would skip them when I would see them on my workout plan.

One particular day I woke up feeling encouraged. I walked in the gym and I told myself that I was going to do dips, even if I had to cry doing them. I went to the dip bars, and once again, I couldn't do them.

As I was struggling to do them, a guy came over and said, "you know that there's a machine that helps, right?" I responded, "A machine?" He showed me a set of machines on the other side of the room, that helped with every workout, in case you had no one to spot you, or you needed the machine to carry some of your weight.

He took me over to the machine and showed me how to adjust the weight. He then said, "the machine will bear the weight that you're unable to bear." I heard the holy spirit whisper to me, "I am your machine." The Holy Spirit is your machine that carries the weight for you. Not only does the Holy Spirit know how much weight you can bear, the Holy Spirit assists you in building your strength and making sure your spirit gets the workout that's needed.

Whatever you're struggling with today, allow the Holy Spirit to spot you, and bear the weight. Even if you feel the pain before you see the results, remember that God's strength is made perfect in our weaknesses.

"Cast your burden on the Lord, and He shall sustain you; He shall never permit the righteous to be moved"
Psalm 55:22

Prayer

Dear God,
Thank you for being my spiritual, personal trainer. I am
grateful for the gift of your Holy
Spirit. Thank you for allowing
me to give all my burdens and
weights to you. Because of you, I
can walk in victory and peace.
In my weakness, your strength is
made perfect, and I accept your
perfect strength. Your joy becomes
my strength, and gives me what
I need to continue my journey of
purpose.

In Jesus' Name,
Amen.

Yeah God! (The Devotional)

It's Your Cake...
Eat It!

I never quite understood the saying, "You can't have your cake and eat it too." If it's mine, why can't I eat it? Eating our cake isn't the problem, not sharing the cake is the problem. God always gives you enough to share with those around you.

In life, we are taught that taking care of ourselves as a priority is being selfish. I subscribed to this thought until one day I was sitting on a plane, and actually listened to the emergency rules. As the flight attendant was giving emergency instructions, I was perplexed by the fact he said, "put the mask on yourself first, then help the person or children, next to you." It changed my perspective. God doesn't want us to treat people better than us, he wants us to treat people as well as we treat ourselves. It's a direct reflection of how you love yourself. You owe it to yourself.

You must be 100% in order to give

others 100%. I don't care if you're a mother, a wife, or whatever else position you hold in people's lives, you must be 100% to be of any good use to others.

The bible doesn't say to love others more than yourself, it says to love others as yourself. We are called to be of service to others, but if you aren't healthy spiritually or physically, you will kill yourself, trying to be a life saver to others.

Prayer

Dear God,
Thank you for revealing to me that you desire for me to be healthy and whole. Thank you for removing the guilt that the enemy sends, when I focus on being spiritually and physically healthy first. I realize that in order to fulfill my calling and assignment to others, I must constantly work on myself. I will continue to walk in your love for me, and use it as a blueprint for loving myself.

In Jesus' Name,
Amen.

Yeah God! (The Devotional)

Losing To Win
Finding Power In Loss

Fantasia Barrino is one of my favorite artists. A few years ago, she put out a song called "Lose To Win." The idea behind it resonated with me. Sometimes you have to lose to win, but it's really not losing, it's sacrificing.

I hate the idea of "losing", because it has such a negative connotation. What about when a loss is really a gain? A moment of loss does not mean you've lost! When Jesus was on the cross, he willingly suffered a temporary loss, and we automatically inherited a win. In church, we always say "he got up with all power in his hand." The truth is, he died with all power in his hand, too.

A loss does not signify a lack of power. Jesus' power never changed, only his situation. Jesus gave up his life without giving up his power, which is why he was able to get up after 3 days. He had to lose his life temporarily, to help us win the victory.

Prayer

Dear God,
Thank you for the power that you've given to me. I thank you that no matter how my situation changes, as long as I have you, I still have power over ever situation I'm faced with. I'm grateful that when I live life with you, even the losses I incur will yield me a win. Your record of winning is undefeated, and I know that because I'm your child, I'm a beneficiary of your winning record, too.

In Jesus' Name,
Amen.

> God's eternal power and character cannot be seen.
> But from the beginning of creation, God has shown
> what these are like by all he has made...
> **Romans 1:20**

Yeah God! (The Devotional)

Authenticity In Identity
Who You Are, Why You Are

Not too long ago, there was a poll on social media, and it asked how you primarily identify. The choices were religion, race, gender, sexual orientation, and a couple of other choices. For me, it was easy, I chose religion. Before I identify as anything else, I identify as a Christian. Why? Because God, my creator, is who gives me identity. He is the only one who can tell me who I am, and how I'm supposed to be.

Social media has a way of making us into who's popular. We become trendy robots and replicas of whoever is the hottest star. At one point, trends were only for fashion, beauty, and health, but now, personalities and artistry have become trends.

It's easy to be defined by society, relationships, friendships, and even family, because they are at the forefront of what influence us. How many people have been influenced by parents, to be or do something different from what they desire? Parents generally want the best for us, but even they don't have the master plan to your life. Purpose only works for you, when you are being you. There's a saying that says, "God can't bless who you pretend to be." So true.

Don't let what you do define who you are. It shouldn't dictate how you feel about yourself. Even your success can trick you into identifying with the wrong thing. How many times have you found your worth in what you do well, or in what people praise you for? In my industry, it's so easy to fall into this. We are praised and paid for our gifts, so it's easy to find your value in that. The dangerous part is when what you do is no longer popular, or necessary. How do you identify then?

I talked to an entertainer whose record sales had recently dropped. Because they primarily identified with their job description, when they were no longer "successful", their identity was lost. He became insecure, he felt threatened by newcomers in the industry, and also became overly sensitive to criticism and correction. He felt that without "success", he was no longer good. He felt pushed out of his field involuntarily. However, many times God forces us out of the old, to get us into the new. The only way to move up, is to first move out and forward.

The truth behind success is that we all have different ideas of what success is. Success can't be found in what you do, success is found in who you are. Simply put, if you are who God called you to be, you're successful. God won't always change what's around you, to keep you where you are. Sometimes he'll change you, to prepare you for where you're going.

You are God's child. Whether you remain popular where you are, or if God moves you on to something new, you are still chosen and you still have a purpose! The bible calls you "God's special possession." Because you belong to God, he is the only one that can give you identity. He will never need the world's help determining what that identity is.

Prayer

Dear God,
Thank you for reminding me who I am. I know that before I was born, I had an identity shaped by you. I will not let anything or anyone define me. I am only defined by you and your word. No matter how my life, career, relationships, or titles shift, I will always be confident in my Christ identity!

In Jesus' Name,
Amen.

> But you are a chosen people, a royal priesthood, a holy nation, God's special possession, that you may declare the praises of him who called you out of darkness into his wonderful light.
> 1 Peter 2:9

Is This Battle Yours?
Hold Your Peace

Every battle is not your battle to fight. Don't waste time fighting a battle that God has already won for you. There are times when we will be required to spiritually roll up our sleeves and fight, but what about the times that we don't? We know we have victory, but it doesn't always feel like it.

I have a friend who grew up in chaos. His home life was full of trauma, toxicity, and turmoil. As we became older, his adult life started to mirror his childhood. He fought everything and everybody. He would date beautiful women who loved him, but he didn't know how to receive love. So he fought. He had great friends, but wasn't used to real friendship. He fought them.

One day he called me, and he poured his heart out. He said he felt like he was still the traumatized child, who fought to protect himself. For all of those years, he fought unnecessary battles. He said to me, "Do you realize how often we fight battles that are already won?" He went on a journey to find God, and today, he's married, he's a father, and he is doing ministry.

The truth is the outside battle had been over, but the internal fight was still on. The issues that we don't get healed from don't go away, they age with us. Ignoring them won't make them go away. We can't move a mountain that we're unwilling to face.

There are a lot of older people who have aged in years, but have yet to hit spiritual puberty. Spiritual immaturity will have you fighting battles that no longer exist. You waste time, energy, and emotions on a fight that never needed to happen. Below are two scriptures for you to keep in mind today. Hold your peace.

> *The LORD himself will fight for you. Just stay calm.*
> *Exodus 14:14*

> *Do not be afraid of them, for the LORD your God Himself will fight for you.*
> *Deuteronomy 3:22*

Prayer

Dear God,
Thank you for fighting for me.
You have promised to go before me, and fight for me. I will
hold my peace, and stand still. I
have no reason to fear, you are a
great warrior, and you will always hold victory in your hand.
Thank you for allowing me to
rest in you and your power. You
are victorious, and because I am
your possession, I have victory,
too!

In Jesus' Name,
Amen.

Yeah God! (The Devotional)

Burn Out
Can It Be Avoided?

Let me start out by saying this, you probably need a vacation. Lol. Most people don't have enough time to reset and refresh. We are so money driven, that we get stuck in that place. Now days, people post things like, "I'll sleep when I'm dead" or "I won't be outworked."

Burn out has affected us all, but sometimes it is misconstrued. It doesn't come from only giving or doing too much. It comes from giving or doing too much in the wrong area. A part of healthy living is giving and doing, but a big part of it is being refilled, too. What's the solution? Take a break.

Jesus even retreated and rested. Mark 4:35-40 chronicles Jesus leaving a crowd of people behind, who all needed him. He gathered his homies, the disciples, and boarded a boat. What did Jesus do? He went to sleep. At other times, Jesus went alone to mountains, to deserts, and lakes. His alone time is where he found restoration, dealt with his emotions, and prayed to his father.

Some people overly work to distract themselves from things that require their attention. Some do it out of greed. Some possibly do it to feel validated or needed. Whatever the reason is, burn out can be detrimental to you and those around you.

It's impossible to be effective when you're feeling burned out. Something will be left undone, or not done with excellence. It's impossible to do anything "as unto God", when you're unable to give your all.

In Ecclesiastes 5:18, we are directed to enjoy the fruit of our labor. It doesn't say enjoy it once you retire, you should consistently enjoy your fruit! I love the 20th verse of this same chapter. It teaches us that when we enjoy what we work for, God keeps us busy with joy, and he distracts us from dwelling unduly on the days of our lives.

Burn out isn't always avoidable, but it is reversible. It doesn't have to last forever. Let's pray about it.

Prayer

Dear God,
Thank you for permission to enjoy life. I know that I get so caught up in working, that I forget I need to experience quietness and solitude. I will follow Jesus' lead, in knowing when to retreat and spend alone time with you. I will not be overwhelmed with the cares of life, but I will run to you. I know that whatever you have me to leave behind, will be taken care of by you. Thank you for restoration. Thank you for the fruit. Thank you for your joy!

In Jesus' Name,
Amen.

Yeah God! (The Devotional)

Transition
The Bridge To Your New Season

Five years ago, I quit a job after more than 10 years of employment. I put all of my belongings in storage, spontaneously jumped in my car, and drove 21 hours from New Orleans to Los Angeles, all by myself. I had no job, no plan...I had only a promise, and people thought I was crazy. However, I knew that God told me to go. Just like my car took me from Louisiana to California, transition did the same for me spiritually.

Transition is your spirit's mode of transportation. When God desires to relocate you, he uses transition to get you there. Transition will continue to happen throughout your lifetime. It's the only way to get to your next season.

Transition is made up of assignments, tests, experiences, lessons and blessings. While seasons add value to your purpose, it's transition that adds value to your life. The strength and wisdom that you gain in transition, will be useful until you leave this earth.

The first indicator of transition is a change in important relationships. When my life began shifting, a lot of my friendships shifted, too. In the natural, when you relocate, you don't take everything with you. There won't always be room for old stuff, people included. The Holy Spirit told me, "it's not personal, it's purposeful." Everyone can't go with you. They'll be fine, and you will be, too.

The second indicator is when the source of your enjoyment changes. The things that you used to enjoy, now irritate you. Things that didn't bother you before, you realize you're not graced to deal with any longer.

Lastly, discontentment or feelings of lack. Many times you won't be able to pinpoint the issue, but you will feel an uneasiness. Transition makes you vulnerable, sensitive, and can be discouraging if you don't stay prayed up. Growing pains are good in transition, because they expose weakness, and reinforce your spiritual framework.

Comfort zones are comfortable, but nothing purposeful grows there! Your transition is divinely orchestrated by God to prepare us, protect us, and promote us. God is with you.

Prayer

Dear God,
I'm grateful for the reminder that you will never leave me or forsake me. Even in transition, I know you are shifting with me. Although I can't see what lies ahead, I have confidence in the fact that you know and that you've already been where I am going. Thank you in advance for showing me where I'm headed, and equipping me for my journey to get there.

In Jesus' Name,
Amen.

The Lord had said to Abram, "Go from your country, your people and your father's household to the land I will show you.
Genesis 12:1

LOSSES

The Unexpected Seeds That Grow

As a child, I remember losing things at school, and going to the "lost and found" to retrieve them. In life, the lost and found, still exists, but in a different form. We'll "lose" things that we weren't ready to part with, or that we thought we would keep forever. However, even your losses produce a harvest.

I started purchasing my first home when I was 23. It was my biggest accomplishment. I spent more than $30,000 to remodel it, and it was a dream come true. After about 3 or 4 years, I ended up "losing" it, and it was the worst feeling in the world. I felt like I had failed, and like a piece of my greatness was lost. One day I prayed, and God shifted my perspective. I heard God say, "a loss is simply an unexpected seed that you've sown."

The lost and found in life exists in different places. You may find what you lost in the form of a lesson, a financial blessing, or maybe even a person. I have a friend who had a miscarriage, all she wanted was to have a baby. She and her husband were crushed when she miscarried. After her loss, she was afraid to get pregnant again. However, a year later, she found out she was pregnant, not with one, but with two babies. That's a harvest!

Even though we lose "things", we never lose the power or ability to get those things. Let that encourage you not to be discouraged by what you lost. Be excited about the harvest that will come, you have the power to reap again.

I don't know what you've lost, maybe a marriage, a job, or time, whatever it is, believe that God will use it to grow something beautiful for you.

Prayer

Dear God,
Today, I change my perspective
on loss. I realize that in your
hands, nothing can become
something. I know that while
I may feel the pain from loss, I
have sowed a seed that will grow
pass what I've lost. Thank you
for reminding me that even in
loss, I'm still powerful and able
to get anything that I've ever
lost, if it's in your will.

In Jesus' Name,
Amen.

Yeah God! (The Devotional)

God...
The Time Machine

How many times have you felt like you've wasted time? You've said to yourself, "if I could turn back the hands of time, I would..." I can confidently say that although God won't turn back the hands of time, I can tell you that he will restore time.

God owns time. As humans, we have a limited understanding that determines how we view time. We set time limits, expiration dates, and we need clocks in order to live. However, God isn't limited to working in the confines of only what we understand.

In Joel 2:25, God said, "I will give you back what you lost to the swarming locusts, the hopping locusts, the stripping locusts, and the cutting locusts. It was I who sent this great destroying army against you."

This verse explains God's promise to restore what Israel lost when their crops were destroyed due to a locust invasion. Imagine not only losing crops, but even the seeds to reproduce!

God can take time out of the equation. God can speed up the time necessary, to receive your blessing. God doesn't need time to add to you. He is the time machine.

Almost 20 years ago, my mom retired from a job she worked for more than 20 years. She had been saying she wanted to go back to school, and get her master's degree, but she felt like she had lost out on that time. Now she had a full time job, and me(I was a full time job all by myself...lol). How could she fit it all in? I will never forget her saying, "I wish I could retire." At 47, we knew that wasn't possible.

A few weeks later she comes home excited. She says that a once in a lifetime opportunity for her to retire has been presented. Her job offered a retirement package to everyone whose age plus years of employment equaled 75. I'm looking at her trying to figure out why she's excited. Her total was less than 70. I will never forget the next words she said. She said, "I'm excited, because they will give you five years of grace on each requirement." Needless to say, she retired that year and now has a master's degree.

God's grace stepped in, and replaced the need for years. Whatever you're waiting on God to do, don't be intimidated by time. God is time.

Prayer

Dear God,
I know that you control time,
and that your grace is sufficient in everything. Thank you
for the promise you've made to
me. I trust that you will restore
time that I've lost. I will continue to walk in your joy, and not
be afraid or intimidated by the
clock of life. I will live at the
pace that you've designed, and
rest in the promise of your peace.

In Jesus' Name,
Amen.

Time For Pruning
How Sweet Is Your Fruit

There are more than 100 scriptures that refer to us either bearing fruit, or comparing us to trees. Like fruit trees, we require pruning to produce properly. Why? Pruning builds the framework for the survival, stimulates growth, and shapes the tree. Pruning ensures that the tree stays strong.

The interesting thing about fruit bearing trees, is that the best time to prune them is during dormancy. Dormancy is the period in an organism's life cycle when growth and development temporarily stops, to help the organism conserve energy. Basically, dormancy is when the organism sleeps. It's also the key time to take steps to prevent the tree from diseases, get rid of insects and eggs, and to give the tree it's nutrients.

As spiritual trees, we must go through that same process to be most effective. We require pruning. There's so much that we accumulate in life, like negative attitudes, generational curses, fears, negative experiences, discouragement, anxiety, unnecessary friendships, soul ties, etc, that serve us no purpose, and have become props in our lives. The cutting away may seem to take away, but really it prepares us for healthy growth and sweeter fruit.

We have all experienced dormant seasons. The seasons where it seems like life is on hold, and nothing in your life is moving. We can all agree that it's easy to get anxious in this state. However, the dormant or "resting" season is the best season that we could go through. Without the dormant season, we wouldn't be prepared for growth, we would be diseased, and we would be limited in our ability to bear fruit.

In this season of your life, allow God to cut away the dead, superfluous parts of you. When you recognize the pruning, you should be excited! The next season after dormancy and pruning, is due season. Get ready to produce the best fruit of your life!

Prayer

Dear God,
Thank you for my pruning season. Forgive me for resisting the pruning process. I know that your desire for me is to produce the best fruit in abundance. I pray that I will never get in the way of you cutting off the unnecessary things in my life. I will let go of it all, and hold tight to your promise. In my dormant season, I will allow your sweet rest to overtake me and replenish me, for my best season yet! You are a good father.

In Jesus' Name,
Amen.

I am the true vine, and My Father is the vinedresser. Every branch in Me that does not bear fruit He takes away; and every branch that bears fruit He prunes, that it may bear more fruit.
John 15:1-2

Yeah God! (The Devotional)

Taking Authority
Losing Control

As humans, we are obsessed with being in control. If we don't have full control, or at least a false sense of control, we are uncomfortable and feel helpless. The truth is that we are never in control. God gave us authority, not control.

So many times as Christians, we speak authority, but we attempt control. It's impossible to enjoy or love what you aim to control. Although, God is ultimately in control, he's not controlling. God seeks willingness and obedience from us, the enemy seeks control of us.

God gave us free will, with the options of having authority or consequences for not utilizing authority. God has placed us in charge on the earth. He has leased us his power and we must be good stewards with it.

How do we utilize our power? Romans 13:1 tells us that there is no authority except from God. We must submit to God. Authority only works when we use it according to God's standard, his way of doing things. When we relinquish our need for control to God, we experience authority in it's abundance.

As a believer in Jesus Christ, authority gives you the power over the enemy, sickness, and disease. Luke 9 & 10 reinforces this and the notion that nothing shall be able to hurt us, because of that same authority.

There's another word that comes to mind, dominion. God has given us dominion over everything on earth. We have permission to rule on earth. Once again, the only catch is doing it God's way. We are made in God's image, therefore, we have to view the earth as he does. We have to care about people, animals, and the environment, just like God does.

There's no complicated set of rules for authority. Just like your home keys allow you access to your home, the keys to the kingdom give you full access to heaven.

Why would you not use the access you've been given? Anything that God said is yours, is yours.

Prayer

Dear God,
Thank you for trusting me with authority. As I let go of the need to know everything, I accept the authority that you have given me to be victorious. I will use my keys to defeat the enemy, disease and anything else that rises up against me. They are no match for you, and as long as I carry you with me, I can overcome them all.

In Jesus' Name,
Amen.

> I will give you the keys of the kingdom of heaven;
> whatever you bind on earth will be bound in heaven,
> and whatever you loose on earth will be loosed in
> heaven.
> Matthew 16:19

Gifts

They Don't Die... They Multiply

Years ago, a young man wanted his parents to buy him a new car. His parents agreed, as long as he finished college. He reminded them of their promise regularly. Four years later, on graduation day, his parents gave him a small gift box. When he opened it, there was nothing but a bible in it. They told him to read Mark 11:23. Irritated, he closed the box, and never opened it again. Years later, he was cleaning up and found that bible. When he opened it, a check fell out, and the memo read, "For your car."

As ridiculous as it sounds for him to not open the gift his parents gave him, that is how we look when God gives us gifts that we refuse to use.

Just like the graduate, we so often get stuck on the way our gift is wrapped or packaged, that we end up forfeiting and squandering what God has given us. The truth was that the bible with a check inside, was just as valuable as the actual car being parked in the driveway. That gift would've given him the ability to walk into the dealership and walk away with the car he wanted.

God has given us all gifts. Maybe it's singing, dancing, acting, leadership, serving others, or whatever else. No matter how you feel about your gift, it can be used, and it is necessary! God doesn't waste gifts on us.

Your gift/talent is a form of currency that God has entrusted us with, no matter how big or small it seems. Just like in Matthew 25:14, we learn about the men with the talents. The important part is not about how much they had, but what they did with what they had. The two who used their talents, doubled what they originally had. The one who hid his talent, ended up with nothing. If you don't use(your gift), you lose! My favorite part of that scripture is the last part, "you've been faithful over a few things, I'll make you ruler over many things." God rewards us when we use what he's given us.

Proverbs 18:16 says, "A man's gift maketh room for him, and bringeth him before great men." Your gifts are currency that opens the door and pays the admission for you to be amongst the great! You will never need a sign from God about using your gift. The gift is all the sign you need. Every gift has an assignment and an audience. God doesn't give us anything that He doesn't want us to use.

Prayer

Dear God,
Forgive me for not using every gift that you have given to me. I will use my gifts, and stand on every promise you've made. I will not hide my talent, or allow myself to be intimidated by the gifts of others. I know that you have given me what I can handle right now, so I will use everything in me. I am grateful that you have promised to reward me for my faithfulness, over what you have given to me. Thank you for every opportunity and platform.

In Jesus' Name,
Amen.

Forgive and Remember...
Never Heard It Put Like That!

I want to start this out by asking, aren't you made in God's image? Hopefully, you answered yes. If so, you have the ability to do and be like him, including forgiving. We've all either said or heard it said, "I forgive, but I won't forget." Is it possible to forget? I personally don't think it's always possible to forget. However, I know it's possible to "remember no more". Hebrews 8:12 says it.

They sound the same, but they aren't. Forgetting is controlled by the brain, implying a literal loss of memory. At times, forgetting is possible. However, more times than not, it's unrealistic to think that all bad memories will be wiped from your brain. What is the answer to forgiving, when you can't forget? Choose not to remember.

"Remembering no more" is an intentional choice to release the pain, even if your mind "remembers" what caused the pain.

Most people would agree that forgiving would be much easier, if we saw the other party suffer as much as we feel like we suffered. Don't stunt your ability to move forward, by waiting to see them suffer. Don't give someone else the power over you being able to move forward.

I'm sure you're asking, "How do I let go of the thing that my mind won't release?" Psalm 103:12 says, "As far as the east is from the west, so far has He removed our transgressions from us." God wants us to do that same thing. You must separate the act from the person. It's not always easy, but it's very possible to love someone without liking what they did to you.

So instead of forgiving and forgetting, maybe the saying should be, "forgive and remember to forget!" When the unpleasant memories come to mind, remember God. Replace your negative thoughts with God thoughts.

Start by keeping your mind on "these things" found in Philippians 4:8. "Whatsoever things are true, whatsoever things are honest, whatsoever things are just, whatsoever things are pure, whatsoever things are lovely, whatsoever things are of good report...think on these things."

Holding grudges is a prideful way of having false power over someone. However, it is a clean heart that forgives what the mind is unable to forget. 1 Corinthians 13:5 tells us that "...love keeps no record of wrong." This is applicable to forgiving yourself, too. Love yourself, keep no records of the wrong and forgive yourself.

One thing that always helps me, is when I literally speak aloud, what I want to feel or experience. When you need peace, open your mouth and speak it! When you want to forgive, open your mouth and speak it!

Lastly, just know that no one can do more to you than you've done to God. Carry his grace. You may have to re-forgive the person, until your heart catches up! The grace they need today, might be the grace you need tomorrow.

Prayer

Dear God,
Thank you for always forgiving me and offering me your grace as a band aid for my wounds. You have established how you want me to forgive, and my desire is to follow you. I pray that when forgiveness becomes hard, you will remind me of myself, so that I may show others the grace that you freely gave to me. Today, I will look for moments to share your love and grace. Today, please forgive me my trespasses, and I forgive those who trespass against me. Your grace is sufficient.

In Jesus' Name,
Amen.

The Cost of Fear

What a price tag...

If fear had a price tag, you wouldn't be able to afford it. Fear is what's most responsible for people missing out on purpose, great relationships, and the best experiences life could offer. I was always taught that fear was the opposite of faith, but what I've realized is that fear is faith...just in the wrong direction. In order to fear something, you have to believe that it has strength, influence, or power over you in some way.

Fear is rooted in our spiritual immaturity, in what we see and hear, and most of all, our past experiences. There's an entertainer who had an extreme fear of flying. It came from a turbulent flight she experienced in the 80s. After that, she never boarded a plane again, which robbed her of opportunities, including going overseas. That's an expensive price tag.

I read an article about starving your fears, and while it was well articulated, I got a different revelation. We can't starve or feed fears. Fear comes from the enemy, which means we can't control it. We can only control our response to it. The key is to not focus on starving fears, but to simply focus on feeding faith. Fear will then suffocate in your presence. You have authority over it.

2 Timothy 1:7 reads, "For God hath not given us the spirit of fear; but of power, and of love, and of a sound mind. The writer laid out a checklist of things to combat fear. First, power. Remember a few days ago, we discussed our authority over the enemy.

Secondly, love. His love for us, and our love for him, casts out fear(1 John 4:17-18). Lastly, God has given us a sound mind, peace. Fear is debilitating, it causes panic, anxiety, depression, amongst other things.

When fear comes upon me, I verbally rebuke the enemy. I recite the scripture, and I command peace and faith to overtake me. "Do not fear" is in the bible more than 80 times. God knew we would constantly need reminders.

Prayer

Dear God,
Thank you for the tools that help me combat fear. You have given me authority over everything that I face, including my fears. I will continue to trust you, and walk in perfect love. I will not allow anxiety, panic, worry, or fear, to rob me of my peace, or any other beautiful moments that you give to me in life. I'm grateful for the victory that I already have!

In Jesus' Name
Amen.

Yeah God! (The Devotional)

God Is Grace

He's in a good mood...

God is in a good mood. Why do we think that God is sitting up in heaven, looking for a moment to punish us? I have a good friend who grew up in a pentecostal church, and they thought everything was a sin. They couldn't watch TV, they couldn't go to a movie theater, and they couldn't listen to secular music. Not only could they not do the above, they thought anyone who did do the above things, was going to hell.

Once we went to college, my friend's entire mentality began shifting. I remember having a conversation and saying, "You do realize God is in a good mood, right?" This revelation of God's disposition changed my life. I realized that many people think that God desires to punish them with harsh outcomes and extreme consequences.

God loves us too much to punish us, for the purpose of hurting us. While God isn't excited to punish us, he is excited to protect us.

A part of God protecting us, is him correcting us. While this might be uncomfortable, it's all for our good. His correction is a reflection of his love, not his mood. He is the epitome of love and compassion. Why would he want to hurt us?

God is love. 1 Corinthians 13:4-8 teaches that love is kind, it doesn't behave rudely, and it thinks no evil, just to name a few. Therefore, God isn't capable of being in a bad mood. Even his wrath doesn't change who He is. In fact, God laughs!

Psalm 2:4 tells us that he laughs at his enemies. God wants us to laugh, too. We are reminded in Proverbs, that laughter is like medicine to the soul. God wants us to enjoy our lives on earth!

Philippians 4:4 says to rejoice in the Lord always. God's joy is the source of our rejoicing. If we are to rejoice always, that means his joy is omnipresent, just like Him. God is consistent. God is good. You have the ability to be just like Him.

Prayer

Dear God,

I want to be a reflection of you and your character. I know that since you created me in your image, I have the ability to be in a good mood and to carry a positive attitude. Thank you for the reminder that you are not looking for a moment to punish me, but you desire to be in constant relationship with me. I love you and I'm grateful that I'm reminded of your compassion, kindness, and joy today. I will rejoice!

In Jesus' Name,
Amen.

Yeah God! (The Devotional)

The Danger of Emotions
Feel & Heal

We all feel them, but do we all heal from them? There is a popular song called *Emotions,* by a group named "H-Town". The lyrics were, "emotions make you cry... sad...glad sometimes." It's true. If you were to rely on your emotions, you would lose it. Emotions are nothing more than a temporary state of mind that is influenced by mood, circumstances, or external factors. We all are born into this world with emotions.

Emotions are our natural and immediate way of dealing with our reality. However, we must be careful. Emotions can impair your judgment, and they can cause you to say, think, or do things that are wrong.

For example, anger is an emotion that has caused damage, through domestic abuse, mental breakdown, and even murder. The bible doesn't say that emotion is bad, but it does tell us not to let emotions cause sin. Ephesians 4:26 tells us to "Be angry, yet do not sin."

Some emotions like happiness and excitement, are positive emotions. Laughter can be the manifestation of positive emotions as well. The bible tells us that laughter is like medicine to the soul. Therefore, emotions can be very useful. However, one of the fruits of the spirit is temperance. Don't allow emotions to gain control of you in the moment.

God knew that we would get emotional, but he still wants us to do the right thing. When you walk in the spirit, you can think soberly, even when you're emotionally intoxicated.

I always say, "everything that deserves your attention, doesn't deserve your emotions." Use your emotions wisely.

Prayer

Dear God,
Thank you for giving me
self-control through your Holy
Spirit. Although I will experience emotion, I know that I
don't have to be a slave to my
emotions. I realize that even in
times of anger, I'm still responsible for doing the right thing,
and not sinning. I will not let
any feeling control me, or cause
me to do or say anything that I
will regret or have to repent for
doing. I thank you that you are
my strength.

In Jesus' Name,
Amen.

Yeah God! (The Devotional)

The Best DIY Project:
YOU

So many times we are able to clearly see and "fix" others, but for some reason, not ourselves. We have the answers, the "what you need to do" advice, and the "I told you so" responses. But, why aren't we as ambitious to work on ourselves? We tend to make other people our projects, but leave the main project, ourselves, undone.

Matthew 7:3 asks us why we see a particle in someone else's eye, but we miss the whole beam in our eye! Isn't it amazing that the scripture implies what needs attention in ourselves, is larger than the small thing you see in someone else? Now, it can be quite uncomfortable to face yourself, but being introspective could potentially change the trajectory of your life.

I see so many "experts" on social media that judge everyone from reality stars to political figures. I always ask what this world would be, if everyone focused on themselves as much as they focused on others?

1 Thessalonians 4:11 says, "Make it your goal to live a quiet life, minding your own business and working with your hands..." Our goal should be to mind our own business. Not only does it help us to be productive, it is what we've been commanded to do.

There is power in minding your business. It allows you to stay focused on what God has put ahead of you, it prevents you from feeling the need to compete with others, and lastly, it keeps you from bearing someone else's load, that you're not equipped to bear.

Galatians 6:4 says, "But let each one examine his own work..." When we focus on our own work, we won't have time for things that aren't our concern. To be clear, that doesn't mean that we shouldn't correct others or care about others, it means that our involvement in the lives of others, should be based on what God has directed us to do. What in your life deserves more attention?

Prayer

Dear God,
Today I make a vow to examine myself, and focus on what you have called me to. I pray that I will always be drawn to honestly look at myself, face the hard truths, and run to your presence to receive the healing and deliverance that I may need. As I focus on myself, I will pray for everyone else around me. Instead of trying to fix them, I will trust that you know best, and will do the work in their lives, as you've promised. Thank you for a fresh perspective.

In Jesus' Name.
Amen.

Yeah God! (The Devotional)

Don't Pray & Worry
It does no good...

I love reading the bible for a few reasons. For one, I love the wisdom and direction that it gives, but secondly, I love the humorous and quick witted delivery, like in Luke 12:25 and 26. It says, "Who of you by worrying can add a single hour to your life? Since you cannot do this very little thing, why do you worry about the rest?" What can we say to that? Lol. It basically told us to get somewhere, sit down, and let God work!

These verses show just how counter-productive worrying truly is. There's nothing that worrying accomplishes, except more worry. I used to always hear old people say, "if you're gonna pray, don't worry. But if you're gonna worry, don't pray." The great thing about God, is that we don't have to carry anything alone.

Matthew 11:28 says, "Come to me, all you who are weary and burdened, and I will give you rest..." God will give you rest.

There are multiple scriptures that speak of God's peace. He has given us his peace, in exchange of our worries. I would say that's a great deal!

It's not always easy, but it's effective. There's a scripture that lists the instructions to getting peace that will guard your heart and mind. Philippians 4:6-7 says, "Do not be anxious about anything, but in every situation, by prayer and petition, with thanksgiving, present your requests to God. And the peace of God, which transcends all understanding, will guard your hearts and your minds in Christ Jesus."

The answer to worry is prayer, petition, and asking God for what you need. If you do this with thanksgiving, God promises to give you his peace that will guard your heart and mind.

You may think you only need to give God the "big" stuff, but give him the little stuff too! Even a leaf will make your arm hurt, if you carry it long enough. Give it all to God! Read Matthew 6:26. We are valuable to God.

Prayer

Dear God,
I will cast my cares and anxiety on you. If you are responsible for the grass growing, the sun shining, and the world turning, then I know you can handle the happenings of my life. Life can be complex and overwhelming at times, but I know that you are always with me and will never leave me. You care about the birds of the air, so I know you are watching me. You are gentle and humble in heart, and I will follow you for the rest of my days.

In Jesus' Name.
Amen.

Yeah God! (The Devotional)

It's Over...
Time To Celebrate!

How many times has something in your life ended, but the pain or sting of it exceeded your excitement for what was next? It could be a relationship, a friendship, or maybe even a job...it's not the end of world.

What if we stopped viewing the ending as an ending, but viewing it as the beginning of something fresh? If I was to think back over all of the dope things that came into my life, it was always after something ended or was completed in my life.

Moving to Los Angeles was the beginning of the best days of my life, but that was only after I closed the chapter of living in New Orleans. It was a little scary, and I could've viewed it as something bad, or even turned around, stayed and missed out on my purpose. Instead, I celebrated the start of something new.

Many times, the only way to welcome new in your life, is to close the door to the old. Don't let it discourage you, don't let it scare you, don't let it intimidate you.

I've experienced a lot of great things in life. I've had to close the chapters to a lot, and some of the chapters closed on their own. Whether you chose to end things, or things ended on their own, I promise you that God will not end anything, without a plan to start the next thing!

You are walking into the best season of your life. As you close out the past 31 days of your life, I pray that something in this devotional has helped you. I'm celebrating with you for the fresh, and new season that you are now walking into! Your latter will be greater!

Prayer

Dear God,
I come to you with excitement and gratitude, welcoming what's next. Thank you for changing my outlook on life, and the never ending freshness that life brings. I will not look at the ending of anything as something negative, but another opportunity to experience your grace, your peace, and your favor. I know that you desire for me to prosper and be of good health, so I will expect that anything that comes into my life, is in alignment with your word! I love you.

In Jesus' Name,
Amen.

TESTIMONY

I know I've passed the 31-day mark, but I felt compelled to add this testimony. I don't know what you're going through or what pain you're currently experiencing, but know that your pain is a sign of life. It's an indicator that your spirit, your mind, and your heart are not paralyzed by the enemy or his plans against you!

One of my best friends' mother suffered a stroke about a year ago. She couldn't walk, she could barely talk, and they weren't sure if she would make it. Every day I would call and check on her. She felt helpless. One half of her body was paralyzed, and she wasn't motivated to use the other side.

She began to be discouraged, and wanted to give up. Well, one day I talked to her, and she preached a sermon...through her pain.

One day we were talking and then she stopped and complained that her leg was hurting. I hollered! She seemed confused and startled. I said, "which leg?" She immediately started crying. The pain was in her "paralyzed" leg. At that point, her pain was an indicator that healing was taking place, and that she wasn't paralyzed.

Her pain in that moment, was a sign of life not only in her leg, but in her body. Pain is an opportunity for God to show himself in your life! Your pain is God's platform. He will use it to bless those around you!